D0604191

STARTING A SPORT

by Harold T. Rober

LERNER PUBLICATIONS ◆ MINNEAPOLIS

Note to Educators:

Throughout this book, you'll find critical thinking questions. These can be used to engage young readers in thinking critically about the topic and in using the text and photos to do so.

Lerner Publications Company
A division of Lerner Publishing Group, Inc.
241 First Avenue North
Minneapolis, MN 55401 USA

For reading levels and more information, look up this title at www.lernerbooks.com.

Library of Congress Cataloging-in-Publication Data

Names: Rober, Harold T., author.
Title: Starting a sport / by Harold T. Rober.
Description: Minneapolis : Lerner Publications, [2017] | Series: Bumba books. Fun firsts | Includes bibliographical references and index.
Identifiers: LCCN 2016022014 (print) | LCCN 2016033144 (ebook) | ISBN 9781512425529 (lb : alk. paper) | ISBN 9781512429305 (pb : alk. paper) | ISBN 9781512427486 (eb pdf)
Subjects: LCSH: Sports—Juvenile literature.
Classification: LCC GV705.4 .R63 2017 (print) | LCC GV705.4 (ebook) | DDC 796—dc23

LC record available at https://lccn.loc.gov/2016022014

Manufactured in the United States of America
1 – VP – 12/31/16

LERNER e SOURCE™

Expand learning beyond the printed book. Download free, complementary educational resources for this book from our website, www.lernerresource.com.

Table of Contents

Let's Play!

Starting a sport is fun.

There are many sports

to choose from.

Players need equipment.

Basketball players

need a ball.

Swimmers need goggles.

What else might you need to go swimming?

Players need safety gear too.

Soccer players wear shin guards.

Helmets keep baseball

players safe.

Why does a baseball player need to wear a helmet?

Some sports are played
by groups of people.

They are team sports.

Baseball is a team sport.

Basketball is too.

Players practice different skills.

Gymnasts learn to tumble.

Golfers learn to hit the ball.

The coach helps players with skills.

The coach teaches everyone how to play the sport.

Players learn a lot from the coach.

What else can a player learn from a coach?

Soon it is time for a game!

Two teams play against each other.

Each team has uniforms.

Uniforms help show

who is on which team.

Each team wears

a different uniform.

Playing sports is great exercise.

It is a fun way to stay healthy!

Sports Equipment

Different sports use different equipment.
Here is the equipment needed to play soccer.

shoes

ball

net

uniforms

shin guards

Picture Glossary

uipment

the objects needed to play a sport

safety gear

gear worn to keep someone safe while playing a sport

ills

things someone learns to do by practicing

uniforms

special clothes worn by a sports team

23

Index

Read More

Binkow, Howard. *Howard B. Wigglebottom Learns about Sportsmanship: Winning Isn't Everything.* Minneapolis: We Do Listen, 2011.

Gleisner, Jenna Lee. *My Body Needs Exercise.* Mankato, MN: Amicus, 2014.

Raatma, Lucia. *Sportsmanship.* Ann Arbor, MI: Cherry Lake Publishing, 2014.

Photo Credits